RECONSTRUCTING
DEMOCRACY

RECONSTRUCTING DEMOCRACY

How Citizens Are Building from the Ground Up

Charles Taylor

Patrizia Nanz

Madeleine Beaubien Taylor

Harvard University Press

Cambridge, Massachusetts
London, England
2020

Library of Congress Cataloging-in-Publication Data

Names: Taylor, Charles, 1931– author. | Nanz, Patrizia, author. |
    Taylor, Madeleine, author.
Title: Reconstructing democracy : how citizens are building
    from the ground up / Charles Taylor, Patrizia Nanz,
    Madeleine Beaubien Taylor.
Description: Cambridge, Massachusetts : Harvard University
    Press, 2020. | Includes bibliographical references and index.
Identifiers: LCCN 2019042310 | ISBN 9780674244627 (cloth)
Subjects: LCSH: Community power. | Political participation. |
    Democracy.
Classification: LCC HM776 .T37 2020 | DDC 321.8—dc23
LC record available at https://lccn.loc.gov/2019042310

CONTENTS

RECONSTRUCTING
DEMOCRACY

Introduction

THERE IS widespread belief in Western societies that our democracies are in trouble. Numerous polls show that people are losing confidence in democracy as a system. Young people in particular think that democracy is a poor form of governance and that an authoritarian or technocratic regime would be a better alternative.[1] At the same time, political developments are causing deep divisions among citi-

1 "Democracy Perception Index 2018," Alliance of Democracies Foundation, Dalia Research, and Rasmussen Global, June 2018, http://www .allianceofdemocracies.org/wp-content/uploads/2018/06/Democracy -Perception-Index-2018-1.pdf.

See also the World Values Survey: R. Inglehart, C. Haerpfer, A. Moreno, C. Welzel, K. Kizilova, J. Diez-Medrano, M. Lagos, P. Norris, E. Ponarin, and B. Puranen et al. (eds.). "World Values Survey: Round Six-Country-Pooled Datafile Version," 2014, www.worldvaluessurvey.org /WVSDocumentationWV6.jsp, Madrid: JD Systems Institute.

Here is the famous, more pessimistic interpretation of Foa and Mounk:

Roberto Stefan Foa and Yascha Mounk, "The Danger of Deconsolidation: The Democratic Disconnect," *Journal of Democracy* 27, no. 3 (July 2016): 5–17, https://www.journalofdemocracy.org/wp-content/uploads/2016/07 /FoaMounk-27-3.pdf.

zens within democratic societies. For example, the vote for Brexit in the United Kingdom and Donald Trump's successful campaign for the US presidency, which invoked nostalgia for a lost past when America was "great," have resulted in xenophobic appeals to exclude those deemed "outsiders." These appeals are directed at those who already feel that society has left them behind.

The erosion of the welfare state and the encroachments of the economic system have opened people's eyes to the fact that they live not only in market economies but in capitalist societies where economic affairs are no longer embedded within social interactions. This separation is essential to the neoliberal policies that have been dominant in recent years. In fact, both democratic politics and various aspects of everyday life have been subjugated to the managerial logic of corporations and banks. The claims made during and after the financial crisis of 2008 that certain banks were "too big to fail" and had to be rescued at all costs, and that there was "no alternative" to the specific conditions that bailout deals presented to Greece and several other countries in the eurozone, severely undermined these democracies. By its very nature democratic politics must always offer more than one avenue out of crises.

Social media and digital communication technologies in general have also played a significant role in the erosion of democratic culture over the last decade. On the one hand, digitalization provides citizens with easy and broad access to information and conveys the impression that their views and actions matter. Initiatives such as www.govtrack.us and @YourRepsOnGuns in the United States, www.theyworkforyou.com in the United Kingdom, and www.openaustralia.org.au in Australia have greatly increased the transparency of political decision-making and enabled like-minded people to build networks and mobilize. On the other hand, the largely anonymous social networks of Web 2.0—together with depoliticized television programming (or pseudo-politicized, in the case of talk shows)—distance citizens from the political sphere. With its focus on finding sympathetic others within "echo chambers" that reject or excoriate dissenting opinion, this form of media consumption acts as a barrier to collective learning and meaningful deliberation. Instead, it provides fertile ground for electronic populism.

In a nutshell, liberal democracies face two major, intertwined problems: the decline of their problem-solving capacities and the gap between political elites and the people. Democratic systems don't deliver better futures (think of environmental policies) not only because lobbies and corporations are so powerful (for example, the car industry or oil lobby), but also because elected officials often don't know which policies are adequate or are afraid to take drastic measures that might not be supported by their constituents. Politicians are afraid to take responsibility because they are not sure what the people want or would accept. Those courageous enough to advance unpopular policies risk the kind of backlash that we see in France with the *gilets jaunes*. This recent protest movement against environmental policy reform in France grew out of the (justified) sense that President Macron's plan to increase taxes on fossil fuels disregarded the dependency of lower-income, rural households on affordable diesel. Soon, right-wing populist politicians like Marine Le Pen managed to channel at least part of the outrage.

Of course, national governments are constrained by political globalization. But they are also limited by global accords such as the Paris Agreement, with its goal of limiting global warming to well below 2°C above preindustrial levels and decarbonizing the global economy to prevent dangerous climate change.

Transformations toward sustainability must be implemented not only at the global level but also through the adoption of sustainable modes of living that can only be developed by politicians at the national and, especially, the local level. It is here that democratic politics needs to be revitalized.

Many people believe that our representative systems have to be reformed, down to changes in the structure and mode of operation of political parties that play a central role in them, and that the excessive power of money in these systems has to be curbed. Others propose reforms in our public spheres, which have become divided as never before in noncommunicating echo chambers created by social media. For example, they suggest the establishment of public platforms as alternatives to Facebook and other social media, or state-controlled platforms to rein in the distribution of deliberately misleading information.

We agree that changes of this kind are necessary, but we would like to add to the agenda of reform. We believe that to restore responsible government we must reconstruct democracy from the bottom up. Only if we enhance and reinvigorate democracy at the base will the citizenry find clarity about what to ask for, or what future to envision for their community or region. Only then can local communities put pressure on their representatives in policy-making bodies to push for more courageous policies.

In this book, we first delineate the challenges faced by local communities and their residents. The degeneration of democracy is strongly connected to the erosion of local communities. For example, localities devastated by deindustrialization, such as those found in the Appalachians or the Rust Belt in the United States or in the Lausitz region in Germany, often become strongholds of xenophobic "populism."

Rebuilding those local communities requires political action that can build new solidarities, align the interests and goals of community members, and set free creative powers to solve complex problems and enable collective agency. In Chapter 2 we look at two kinds of action: first, self-organization at the local level—which may or may not have the same boundaries as a unit of local government—in order to find a consensus on the needs and goals of the community, and ways to bring these to fruition; and second, modes of government-initiated consultation with ordinary citizens, who will often have no official office or function in government at any level, again with the aim of defining common goals. We introduce various examples of successful community organizing and consultation to better understand how democracy can be reconstructed from the bottom up. In the final part of the book we will return to the mechanisms by which the remaking of local political communities can work to reconstruct and renew democracy as a political system.

CHAPTER 1

Remaking the Local Community

RECONSTRUCTING OUR DEMOCRACIES must begin from the bottom up. This means changing the way local communities respond to their troubles and grievances. Effective responses in practice would mean something like this: various representatives of local societies and organizations—chambers of commerce, churches, local associations, or just people who want to take an active part—come together with a view to determining how they can cope with their situation, often a deteriorating one. They try to elaborate a plan, say, how to find new forms of employment where older or more traditional ones are beginning to fail.

Currently many local communities do not respond effectively to new challenges. We find a classic example of this problem in Western countries which realize that, in order to cope with global warming, they have to scale down their coal extraction, such as in the Appalachian region in the United States, or Brandenburg and Upper Saxony (the Lausitz region) in Germany. It also exists in the rust belts of the United States and France, where a mixture of competition from newly industrializing societies and from automation has undercut local industries. In all these cases, the regions have been devastated for decades by deindustrialization, neoliberal fiscal policies, and political neglect such that they find themselves lacking the resources to effectively respond to their present and future challenges.

These communities lack not only financial means and political influence, but also resources, which are sometimes even harder to obtain because they cannot simply be transferred from one part of society to the other, as the German government is attempting to do in the Lausitz by channeling huge amounts of money into the region. The resources and skills we have in mind instead belong to social capital or culture.

Industries like coal, steel, or manufacturing have shaped not only the skills and income of large parts of the population but also the culture of the region, such as the prevailing images of what it means to be a worker or what it means to care for your family.

With deindustrialization these communities have also partly lost, among other things, their self-esteem or their sense of self-worth, on both the individual and the collective level.

Often hand in hand with the loss of self-esteem resulting from economic decline, such communities have also lost their sense of political efficacy. Politicians have preached global free trade and neoliberal labor-market reform and have promised that the rewards would eventually "trickle down" to all households. But in the Lausitz or the Rust Belt, decline has been steady for decades now, so that people have lost their faith in the political system, feeling more and more like passive victims of an anonymous machine. Those who are able to leave for the urban centers do so, while those who remain retreat to the private realm.

In effect, the local community loses its capacity to self-organize and to develop new ideas to move forward. It also loses its capacity to effectively lobby its representatives, so that a vicious self-reinforcing cycle is set into motion: the political inefficacy of the communities feeds back and reinforces the original erosion of the local political community. This results in a fundamental decline in voters' understanding of the mechanisms of change, of how they might collectively take their fate into their own hands and move on. It's clear that this "Appalachian" kind of predicament will become increasingly common. Not just coal is at stake, but also oil, for instance in the Alberta oil patch. The rest of Canada is becoming more and more hostile to oil pipelines, partly out of a sense of the dangers they pose to the environment when there's a spill, and partly out of the general sense that we have to get away from carbon-generated energy. At the same time, rust belts continue to develop owing to competition from the third world, as well as from automation, particularly with the striking new developments in artificial intelligence. The erosion of local communities deeply affects the political systems of our current democracies, as we will now explain.

What we've called here a decline in voters' understanding of the mechanisms of change is part of a wider phenomenon of disconnect between the needs and aspirations of ordinary people and our system of representative democracy. Modern democracies, unlike ancient Greek poleis, have to operate through representative institutions. Replacing these entirely with direct democracy is not an option. But at the same time, for democracy to *really* work, there has to be a continued connection between these institutions and the goals and requirements of citizens. Unfortunately, this connection can fray, and even break, for a number of reasons.

First, the agenda of modern societies is vast and diverse. Governments not only manage our economies in a globalized world but also finance and administer welfare systems, decide important issues concerning marriage and family life, pursue foreign policy goals, and so on. Not all of these can be salient all the time; and what decides their saliency or their recession from public attention is largely how they figure in the public sphere, particularly in the major media. The vital needs of some citizens can be relegated to the sidelines because other issues dominate public discussion. This is what has happened in many Western countries recently in relation to the skewed distribution of the economic benefits of free trade and globalization. It took the menace of "populist" electoral success against mainstream parties for this issue to take center stage.

Second, money is very powerful in democratic polities. It affords some individuals control of the media and underpins the skewing of attention just mentioned. It can also function more directly through lobbies and the financing of election campaigns, as we see perhaps most vividly in the United States today.

Third, in recent decades, neoliberal illusions about the nature of markets, and their supposed benign operation to secure fair distributions of new wealth, have obscured some of the most blatant inequalities, or underplayed their significance, on the grounds that things will work out in the end.

The last two trends have contributed to a development that many describe as the present crisis of liberal democracy in the West. The rise of right-wing populist movements, both in Europe and in the United States, constitutes a serious challenge to the egalitarian, open democracy that we have been trying to construct throughout the postwar period, which embodies the core values of both the American republic and the European Union.

The more spectacular feature here is the growth of xenophobia, suspicion of the outsider, and resistance to migration, even of desperate refugees. No doubt what has contributed crucially to these movements has been a widespread sense among working and middle classes in many countries that their standard of living has been falling; that after the prosperity of the postwar years (what the French call *Les Trente Glorieuses*), they have lost ground; that they, and even more so their children, face downward social mobility, with a dearth of good, steady jobs; that they face a world, in other words, where jobs will be scarcer, more temporary, and more precarious.

In fact, the workings of globalization and automation, in a context of laissez-faire neoliberalism, then exacerbated by the financial crisis of 2008 and rendered more severe by politics of austerity, have together brought about a massive increase in inequality. And they have produced a great downgrading in the rust belts and small towns of a number of countries, notably the United States and France. This feeling of having been downgraded has pushed many people in these regions to vote for the illusory and discriminatory politics of Donald Trump, Marine Le Pen, and the like.

Indeed, the objection formulated against mainstream parties is that they have given preference to "outsiders," mainly immigrants or refugees, over the "real" (French or American) people. And even in societies where the economy is in much better shape and employment is still high, like Germany, similar reproaches are leveled against the traditional major parties: specifically, that they prioritize refugees at the expense of meeting the needs of Germans.

The decline in ordinary voters' understanding of the mechanisms of change in recent decades was clearly crucial to the success of populist movements like the Trump candidacy, the Front National in France, and the AfD in Germany. It doesn't matter how you explain the success of extraordinary appeals to "make America great again" or the like by restoring an impossible past, whether you suppose that the voters are too ignorant to see through such simple remedies or you suppose that they do indeed see how hopeless they are as remedies, but in their frustration are eager to make a gesture that shocks bienpensant elites. All that matters is that this desperate rhetoric could begin to recruit voters only once they had lost the sense that they could effectively promote their needs and interests through the democratic process.

The disconnect to the citizenry we're describing has grave consequences and has to be reversed. But these developments also should convince us that a reconnection will not automatically come about through the everyday workings of our democratic societies.

Nor will it be enough (but still, of course, necessary) to just go on deflating the myths about the dangerous outsider, particularly Islamophobic fantasies that paint all Muslims as potential terrorists. We will not win the battle against xenophobic populism without tackling the justified sense of neglect felt by many working- and middle-class people. We have to act decisively to bring their needs and aspirations to bear on our representative institutions again.

Reconstructing democracy from the bottom up is one important measure to do this. It is not the only step we have to take, but it can be an important part of the solution, as we show in Chapter 3; where a local public can, at one and the same time, clarify the programs they need, and create solidarity around these programs, they can become a political force that representatives (at least on a local level) must listen to. A new and powerful link is created between local needs and aspirations, and the democratic system.

Or we could put it another way: the political sphere, in Hannah Arendt's sense of an open deliberation among equal citizens about their common goals and action, will have suddenly been enlarged to include not only deputies in Parliament, but also the new group of informed and engaged citizens. It is projects that enable the expansion of the political that we shall be looking at in this book.

Before we address the question of how remaking local communities might have salutary effects for the wider political system, we must look closely at the starting point: What would a reconstruction of democracy from the bottom up look like in communities such as those of the Rust Belt, the Appalachians, or the Lausitz? How would the remaking of local communities enhance their ability to cope with the hazards of deindustrializing societies? How would it support the renewal of democracy as a political system more broadly?

Now this kind of self-organization is already happening in a number of local communities today.[1] But we need a lot more of these communities, and, as we have seen when portraying regions like the Lausitz

---

1 For example, Thomas L. Friedman, "Where American Politics Can Still Work: From the Bottom Up." *New York Times,* July 3, 2018.

See also recent local economy initiatives in the United States: "Local Economy Framework," BALLE, accessed January 20, 2019, https://bealocalist.org/local-economy-framework/.

or the Rust Belt, we usually need to start with the question of how to initiate and foster the process from the outside when it is badly needed and yet isn't happening. For instance, a government may determine that it needs to close a coal mine and will try to bring the local community on its side for this measure, which is dictated by the urgent battle against global warming.

This is a daunting task. First of all, it requires finding and making contact with local people who are already asking the crucial questions; to continue with our example, this means people who realize that coal can't go on forever as a source of employment, and that the region needs some alternative economic solution that can generate jobs. Second, these people have to find each other (or be put in touch with each other).

Then begins the hard task of working out what such an alternative might be. This is where input and insight from the local community become essential. Outsiders might have some good ideas about alternative economic vocations for the region, but these cannot get off the ground unless they somehow resonate with the local community. This is not just a matter of their economic promise; the proposed line of work, production, or service provision must make sense in terms of the skills and capacities of the region, as well as its identity.

For example, one of the great obstacles facing any alternative to coal mining in the Lausitz area of Brandenburg, Germany, is the strong sense of coal mining as a historic identity, with its image of successful struggle against obstacles and difficulties—even heroism—which surrounds the miners' vocation with a powerful aura. (Something similar may be found in Appalachia, say, in West Virginia; Trump exploited this in his campaign.)

Finding a solution—a vocation that both has promise economically in relation to the larger society and also can speak to the community itself—is a task that neither insiders nor outsiders can resolve alone. Here's where someone from the outside with experience in such a process of deliberation and consensus building can be an important resource. Such a person should have some idea of what realistic options might be, but their task would be to facilitate discussion, exploring various possibilities in search of meaningful, "resonant" options.

In short, this person would function as what is known in French as an *animateur*. The person concerned would need special skills analogous to those that ethnographers develop: the ability to listen deeply and eventually come to understand the particularities of the local situation, the terms, and the reference points of local identities. Articulating these particularities may require forging terms that are not already available in established social science disciplines. It requires a certain kind of sensibility to recognize the differences, as well as the powers of articulation to find / recognize the right words, the key terms.

If we think of the typical situation faced by local communities when a major employer pulls out, we can reason through to the necessity of the kind of bottom-up community organizing that the Incourage community foundation engages in in the United States. We return to this organization below.

What do you need for this kind of bottom-up community organizing? First, you need certain facts about the external and internal environments, such as new economic possibilities which could be viable in the region, and an inventory of skills and capacities of the local population: those they already have, and those they can easily acquire.

But this is not enough. Second, people must express their needs and find clarity about their aspirations, or what they would ideally want to do. These are, in fact, important constituents or determinants of the first point above.

But it is not enough to learn these things from the outside. Third, they have to be established in conversation with the people concerned. Some aspirations will only emerge in the exchange, and only the people concerned can identify common goals through this conversation. This kind of mutual encounter and discussion helps generate the common purpose essential for planning the future of the community, while at the same time generating the sense that everyone is on the same side, overcoming differences and generating trust. Everybody has to not only be heard, but also *feel* heard.

We look into the details of such processes shortly in Chapter 2. But we can already see how such deliberation, once it has started to work, can generate the preconditions for its own expansion and consolidation and can thereby become the engine of a reconstruction of democracy from the bottom up. Once people come together in this way, important change can happen. We distinguish four different building blocks of this change:

(1) It involves an existential shift in stance: From a sense that we as a community are the victims of powerful

forces beyond our control, such as the "globalizing elites" or "distant technocrats," or the disloyal competition of foreigners, we come to see ourselves as capable of taking initiative, of doing something to alter our own predicament. Therefore, the emergence of a deliberative community, of the "political" in Arendt's sense, generates *an empowering consciousness of collective agency and possibility* among the local community.

(2) At the same time, the fact that we have to join forces and work with others, from different organizations, confessions, outlooks, and even political convictions, makes us listen to each other; we now have a stake in working out something together with these others. We can't sit back and simply criticize or demonize them. Face-to-face contact often softens our stereotypical hostilities toward each other. Thereby, deliberative communities *build new inclusive solidarities and trust* among the participants.

(3) Once we come together, we also *open up new alleys to creativity.* We might even bring about what has been called "breakout innovation." The thesis of Cea and Rimington is that genuinely innovative solutions often emerge, not from closed-door, top-down processes, but from inclusive processes in which a large number of diverse actors involved in the activity or

community, including those whose lives are conditioned or impacted by it, take part in planning and decision-making from the beginning.[2] The idea of "creating breakout innovation" through wide co-creative processes reflects elements of the same promise that we foregrounded in number 1 above: namely, a realignment of both knowledge and motivation, both a clearer vision and shared power around this vision. Notably, technical innovations also seem to come about most readily in trustful and co-creative exchanges among people of diverse backgrounds.[3]

(4) Once we have gone through the common discussion and once we have come up with some plan, such as how to find new avenues of employment, or modes of retraining, or new kinds of service to the community, our standing as a group has significantly changed. Our interpretation and understanding of the situation, our interests and goals, and even our motivations, values, and vision have become aligned. Now we are in a position to know what we must de-

2 Joanna Levitt Cea and Jess Rimington, "Creating Breakout Innovation," *Stanford Social Innovation Review* (Summer 2017): 31–39.

3 Elvire Meier-Comte, Knowledge Transfer and Innovation for a Western Multinational Company in Chinese and Indian Technology Clusters (Augsburg: Rainer Hampp, 2012).

mand of higher levels of government—of the central governments on the one hand, and the level of state in the United States, province in Canada, or Land in Germany on the other. We not only know what to demand, but in virtue of having a program based on a strong local consensus, we inevitably have some greater political clout. The elected representatives for our area, on both the state (or province) and the federal level, have a strong incentive to listen, or at least to take account of this program in some way. Once a responsive connection to the political system has been successfully established, we feel empowered because we *are* empowered. Because of its potential for the *alignment of goals, knowledge, and motivation,* the rebuilding of local deliberative communities is both a mode of organization and a means of political mobilization.

On the one hand, effective community action *requires* these four building blocks as a prerequisite to change. To make people meet, share information, build new understanding, create new knowledge together, establish common goals, and so on, requires a minimal existing baseline of all four elements. But, on the other hand, once you have put those building blocks into place, they will sustain themselves. They will even generate their own dynamics of expansion because they are resources that are not depleted when they are used in effective community action but rather are enhanced by such use.

In the following pages, we look at a number of examples of projects in which such creation of novel programs winning wide assent has been successfully carried through. We are not trying to look at the gamut of forms that participatory democracy and community organization can take. Interesting as this would be, it is beyond our scope. We offer a brief overview of this wider field. But our main interest lies in projects that do pioneering work in creating novel programs or establishing new forms of solidarity. We tell stories we know well about successful examples of experiments of revitalizing democracy from the bottom up.

This means, in the realm of political participation, that we are less concerned with examining situations in which an already well-formed question is being decided with significant input from citizens at the base—as, for instance, when ordinary citizens are given a say in shaping the municipal budget (as in

Porto Alegre), or in deciding where a new facility will be situated. In the projects we discuss, the crucial questions will be open-ended ones, such as the familiar search for a viable alternative economic role for a rust belt region, or the attempt in a run-down quarter of a city to find a way to build a place with which people can identify, and to which they are happy to belong. In many of these cases, the successful solution ultimately worked out was not—even sometimes could not have been—imagined at the start by the people concerned. This is why Bruno Latour, in the face of the many symptoms of the current crisis in France, warns the French government to limit the topics and questions of the "grand debate" initiated with the citizens.[4]

Similarly, in the field of community organization, we do not look at many important attempts to mobilize citizens, such as the forms of neighborhood organization pioneered by Saul Alinsky, which aim to achieve certain defined goals and which are still being carried on today.[5] The enterprises in this domain that we look at have wider-ranging and less fully defined

4 Bruno Latour, "Passer de la plainte a la doleance," *Le Monde,* January 10, 2019.

5 Luke Bretherton, *Resurrecting Democracy: Faith, Citizenship, and the Politics of a Common Life* (Cambridge: Cambridge University Press, 2015).

goals; they aim not only to achieve certain defined goals but also to increase citizens' capacity to undertake a wide range of goals in the future.

Thus, the projects that are our main objects of concern are ones whose purposes are more complex and less easily defined beforehand, in the hope that this narrowing can nevertheless yield important insights, because the projects we discuss fulfill a role, crucial in today's democracies, of enlarging the range of viable answers to the looming challenges and dilemmas of our global societies.

But our selection of examples is restricted in another sense, too, of course: Our focus here is limited by the experience and expertise the three of us possess. Others could add considerably to the list and widen the reflection. But the focus on the American scene, and on the European context, reflects our experience.

CHAPTER 2

Helping to Rebuild
Political Communities

LET'S LOOK AT SOME examples of the kind of
open-ended innovative projects that we described in
Chapter 1. Several in Europe and the United States are
worth examining.

Langenegg is a linear settlement in Austria near
the Swiss border with a population of 1,100. At one
time local youths deserted Langenegg in search of
work elsewhere, and shops in the village center closed
one by one as life in the area ground to a halt. The
mayor commissioned several studies, leading to the
development of various strategies to halt rural flight
and guide demographic change. But nothing seemed
to work.

Finally, an experiment was launched using a simple process that empowered citizens to control the transformation of their village. Fifteen randomly selected residents were invited to join the process in its early stages. At their first meeting, instead of drawing up a list of changes that they wished to see, the participants talked about the positive aspects of life in Langenegg, such as the fact that staff at the local bakers still addressed their customers by name and that those citizens who worked locally were able to spend more time with their families because they didn't have to commute. The group prepared a list of people who contributed to the quality of life in the village. The list identified two hundred individuals who were then celebrated at a local festival. The group began to grow in the months that followed as more and more people joined the transformation process. A small and diverse coordination team was established. The mayor abstained from joining this body, allowing active citizens to take the lead.

Twenty years have passed since then and much has happened in Langenegg. Over time self-organization has been systematically embedded in local planning and led to a successful structural change. Local businesses have survived and thrived; a village shop has opened together with a hotel and a café next to the village day care center. New employment opportunities have emerged with the founding of a social enterprise and a nursing facility. Langenegg's population is growing steadily. Citizens have embraced sharing as a way of life, establishing sharing mechanisms for cars, seasonal travel passes, and e-bikes. With its numerous photovoltaic and solar power systems and biogas plants, Langenegg has also pioneered energy self-sufficiency, and in 2010 the village was presented with the European Village Renewal Award. Langenegg is not an isolated case. There are many similar examples at the local and regional levels.

For another example, we turn to a community in the United States that is still in a process of evolution, but has already made significant headway. The community is South Wood County (SWC), Wisconsin, and it faced a crisis when the large paper mills that had been the mainstay of the economy for more than a century began to downsize after 2000. Nearly 40 percent of local employment was lost by 2005. Jobs at the paper mills declined 35 percent between 2000 and 2010. And then the largest locally owned factory was sold to a multinational corporation and production was further reduced.

People looked for new jobs in manufacturing, but there were few; the jobs that were available typically required a different skill set from what most locals possessed. The lack of jobs was bad enough, but the withdrawal of the major sources of employment also deprived the community of some of their traditional leaders, because mill executives had served as public officials and benefactors. This is where Incourage, a local community foundation with a mission to model participatory approaches to place-based development, stepped in to try to remedy the situation. The foundation understood that the best and most sustainable solution was for community members to come together and elaborate a common solution. But for this to happen, new channels of communication between residents had to be created.

Residents had relied on the *Daily Tribune* and a local radio station as the main sources of local news for decades. The *Tribune* originally had a paid circulation of fourteen thousand, but after 2000, a new publisher bought the paper and gradually reduced local news to a single page. Soon local circulation was down 63 percent. At around the same time, a widely read company paper disappeared when the company downsized. The nearest TV channel largely ignored Wood County events. How could a high level of awareness of local news be brought back? And how could greater intercommunication between residents be established?

Incourage hadn't originally imagined that it would have to meet these challenges in order to make headway in its main goal of helping a community consensus take shape. But these obstacles to the circulation of news and ideas turned out to be an important roadblock. The obvious solution seemed to be to start communicating online, but it turned out that a third of lower-income families didn't use the internet. Incourage somehow needed to start closer to the ground to catalyze community involvement. Incourage organized focus groups of more than eighty residents who helped develop solutions to address community information challenges, such as "tech days" promoted by a local volunteer. The same person later gathered information about the demand for computer classes in her area, and then worked with library leaders and the foundation to create them.

In a 2013 case study about Incourage's work in SWC, one Incourage employee recalled that she "saw folks go from small (not believing their ideas made a difference) to big (my ideas can make a difference and I want to learn more)." The same employee noted that catalyzing this "virtuous circle" is a crucial component of Incourage's work because it challenges old habits of disengagement. Incourage CEO Kelly Ryan commented that "it is promoting culture change—residents begin to understand that they have power and can make a difference."[1]

In this way, a society with strong intercommunication can be built at the base, starting with single capillaries, but building on the self-confidence they create to multiply at an ever-faster rate. Fostering communication, even on a small scale, like a focus group, can have important consequences for the larger community. This "flywheel effect" results when a small but targeted investment of energy creates momentum for broader change.

To address pressing workforce issues, Incourage invested deeply in creating Workforce Central, a Na-

---

[1] These and other observations of community members may be found in this case study prepared by FSG and Network Impact for the John S. and James L. Knight Foundation: FSG and Network Impact, *Case Studies: How Four Community Information Projects Went from Idea to Impact,* February 2013, https://www.knightfoundation.org/reports/case-studies.

tional Fund for Workforce Solutions site and a multisector workforce training initiative to serve SWC businesses and workers. The early focus groups helped the foundation identify gaps in how organizations that served job seekers shared information with one another and with potential workers. To fill these gaps, Incourage connected local agencies, organizations, and businesses so that they could share information on how education and support services for job seekers can be more efficiently aligned with employer needs. Thus, the foundation began to intentionally map and use information in its local change work.

Results have included simple solutions, such as an agreement from the city of Wisconsin Rapids to lower transportation costs for trainees who attend classes at a local technical college, and more complex collaborations, such as the launch of a new shared curriculum on specific training for locally available jobs. Greater understanding of the link between access to information and job growth has also prompted Workforce Central partners to incorporate digital literacy into credential training for under- and unemployed workers, including former mill workers with limited computer skills.

Connected with this work, Incourage hosted over seventy-five community conversations that included more than five hundred participants. "Several people in the community conversations came from organizations that I had not seen participate before," observed one resident, echoing other participants' surprise that their less-involved neighbors and friends attended public meetings.[2]

Importantly, the process of gathering and sharing information seems to have positively affected local norms of civic engagement. More than 4,100 residents completed a 2012 community survey, with 59 percent of respondents indicating that they were interested in future discussions to develop a community plan. The overwhelming response rate for the survey demonstrated that large numbers of SWC residents felt ready to contribute to a broad-based community process. One resident noted that "five years ago, this kind of thing would have been unthinkable," while another resident, upon hearing that more than four thousand people took the survey, observed, "We feel now that we need to make things happen. Before, we felt like someone else would take care of it."

---

2 FSG and Network Impact, *Case Studies.*

"What we learned along the way," Kelly Ryan remarked, "is that information has its own ecosystem and reflects the culture of a community . . . in order to upend a culture that is paternal, dependent and with a strong sense of entitlement, you have to include information in your change strategy."[3]

Incourage saw the potential in community conversations and moved to channel resident engagement into a new participatory planning process. The foundation had purchased the Tribune building, a large property in a downtown area that the *Daily Tribune* newspaper had vacated when it downsized. The best use of the facility, which was located on a section of riverfront once dominated and controlled by paper mills, would be decided by residents themselves.

The "Tribune process," as it is now known, engaged more than two thousand people in SWC over three years. Incourage trained residents as community organizers to facilitate resident conversations and hired the firm Concordia to guide the community's decision-making and planning. Concordia had an established track record in Louisiana and other regions in the United States, incorporating local knowledge and experience into community planning processes.

---

3 FSG and Network Impact, *Case Studies.*

Open to all residents, the planning process itself took place in an elder services center close to the Tribune site. To encourage broad participation, childcare was made available, food was served, and meetings were held in the evening or at other times of day that were convenient for residents. This attention to residents' needs and preferences was essential to the continuity and success of the process.

Early discussions established a set of core considerations for the planning process. Residents agreed on the overarching relevance of several factors in addition to the need for local economic growth: the value and importance of relationships and human potential, creativity, knowledge, and innovation. These considerations became touchstones in setting priorities and making trade-offs.

An initial phase of planning determined how the building would be used. Included in the final plan were a culinary kitchen, an art studio, a creative workshop, and community meeting rooms, as well as open spaces. The plan also included a microbrewery—inspired in part by regional economic data showing that production of specialty beers had the potential to expand in central Wisconsin—and a recreational rental facility next to the Wisconsin River. The river, which had primarily served as a "working river" for the mills, was now incorporated into Tribune planning as an environmental asset.

Concordia's role in the process was key. First, there was no local capacity to facilitate a protracted, multipronged, resident-centered process such as this. Second, Concordia staff members were accepted by residents as third-party actors with no "agenda." The role of resident community organizers who served as facilitators of small group discussions was also important. Expert outsiders who offered advice during the process could be perceived as purveyors of ideas that were alien or far-fetched. Resident facilitators of small group discussions ensured that nuances were explored in language that residents could understand and that final decisions were made on residents' terms.

Concordia partnered with Incourage to bring several outside experts into the process, mainly to infuse reliable information into decisions that required a level of technical knowledge that local participants didn't have. This was the case with deliberations around the building's energy efficiency features. High turnout to hear an invited speaker discuss environmental sustainability and its importance to communities created a critical mass of support among residents. Despite the higher construction cost, participants voted to include items in the final design that met the highest Leadership in Energy and Environmental Design (LEED) standard, including biophilic elements, efficient fixtures, passive design features, and solar panels. Consensus among resident planners was that the building should serve as a model of sustainability, the first of its kind in the community.

Fundraising for the Tribune is still ongoing, with plans for construction soon. But as a banner above the site reads: "The Tribune is not just a Building." Incourage's intention from the start was to maintain momentum toward a more informed and engaged community. Early signs indicate that the process is having that flywheel effect. Starting from the traumatic widespread disappearance of traditional jobs, through the early work of opening information channels and supporting Workforce Central and the project of the Tribune building, the SWC community made strides to acquire agency in designing its own future. Some of this is reflected in the results of a survey administered to participants a year after the planning was complete. The survey asked residents about the Tribune process and how it had affected them.

Many respondents reported that, as a result of their participation, they met another resident for the first time or shared news or other information with another resident. More than half of respondents reported that they received or accessed more local information, or strengthened a connection or made a new friend in the community. Residents also reported that as a consequence of their participation they had an increased sense of responsibility to do their part to make their community a better place to live. One in five residents said they had contacted an elected official, and one in six said they had joined or started a new civic initiative as a result of the process. One respondent observed, "Residents are asking more relevant questions about why things are or are not happening. I am noticing that more residents are feeling like their showing up and providing input actually matters."

Residents also expressed greater optimism about the future of their community as well as increased pride in their community as a consequence of their participation. This is a positive signal that the Tribune process along with other, similar interventions will have a long-term impact on SWC's future. A three-year study conducted by Gallup in twenty-six communities across the United States has shown that citizens' pride and level of optimism in their community correlate with their level of community attachment, and that community attachment correlates strongly with local GDP growth.[4]

The Tribune process was a carefully planned effort to activate residents at the base while converting a visible sign of the area's decline into a lasting symbol of shifts underway. It is also a good example of a place-making strategy that taps into people's desire to connect socially with others in communal, culturally resonant spaces. It is not a coincidence that many successful organizing efforts start with a physical space.

In an urban area of San Diego known as Market Creek Plaza, low-income residents from diverse ethnic backgrounds have joined with a local nonprofit to develop a cultural and commercial hub in their neighborhood. The impetus was decades-long underinvestment in the area, not the loss of local manufacturing jobs. But the SWC and San Diego cases are related. In both instances, the process aimed to reclaim neglected space for community benefit while under-

---

4 "Soul of the Community," Knight Foundation, accessed February 20, 2019, https://knightfoundation.org/sotc.

writing broad-based resident engagement in community change.

The "how" in our San Diego example starts with the Jacobs Family Foundation (JFF) in partnership with the Jacobs Center for Neighborhood Innovation (JCNI), groups committed to supporting a resident-centered process of development in San Diego's Diamond Neighborhoods. At the time, some 88,000 residents speaking more than fifteen languages lived in the Diamond. The median household income was $32,000, compared to $46,000 in San Diego as a whole, and nearly a third of households survived on less than $20,000 annually. JCNI believes that for neighborhood revitalization to be successful, residents must own the process of development and the assets of all projects. In the context of Market Creek Plaza, this meant organizing the initial financing of the project but also facilitating resident participation in the planning, decision-making, implementation, and ultimate ownership of the project in a literal economic sense. Making Market Creek Plaza a reality involved several steps over a period of six years.[5] JCNI organizers began with neighborhood outreach and

5 Our summary of the Market Creek Plaza process draws from a case prepared by PolicyLink for the Jacobs Family Foundation: Lisa Robinson, Judith Bell, Raymond A. Colmenar, and Milly Hawk Daniel,

relationship building. They sent a survey to residents and organized meetings with local business owners to learn what they wanted to see at the site. Residents also helped shape the project in visioning sessions and strategy meetings facilitated by JCNI's outreach team. Together, this input would inform the guiding vision for Market Creek Plaza's development.

JCNI also ensured continuing resident participation by creating and supporting ongoing teams of residents in the substantive work of the project. Teams were cross-cultural and assisted in the strategy, design, and implementation of various areas of the work. The teams also linked Market Creek Plaza to wider community networks. Valuing residents' time and knowledge, JCNI paid stipends to members of teams who were directly involved with day-to-day implementation. Teams started in large gatherings to develop a shared vision for a specific aspect of the project then divided into smaller teams to oversee implementation. Community teams oversaw each aspect of the project from art and design to business development and leasing.

Market Creek Plaza: Toward Resident Ownership of Neighborhood Change: A PolicyLink Case Study, (Oakland, CA: PolicyLink, 2005).

In order to build skills in the community, JCNI facilitated multiple training and capacity-building opportunities for residents including minority construction contractors and emerging entrepreneurs. To help entrepreneurs strengthen their existing businesses or take their business concept to a workable plan, JCNI provided hands-on technical assistance as well as access to low-cost capital through a partnership with a local small business development corporation.

As in the case of SWC's Tribune process, residents in the Diamond participated directly in the project's design and implementation. However, Market Creek Plaza took this ownership concept one step further by fostering direct economic ownership of the site. To make individual ownership a reality, residents were able to buy "units" in the development through an Initial Public Offering.

Today, Market Creek Plaza extends over ten acres and includes several locally owned restaurants, a large grocery store, a fitness center, and an open-air amphitheater. An outdoor public art collection—mosaics, totems, and murals—in combination with the architecture of Market Creek Plaza's buildings reflects the artistic traditions of the diverse ethnic and cultural groups in the neighborhood.

This creating of place is essential to humans. Places (*topoi, loci*) are defined by what exists there. One place is "on the mountain," another is "by the river," another "in the meadow." Human beings exist first and essentially in places; that is, these have meanings for us. Being "in the forest" is different from being "in the city." And within cities themselves, places differ; a dormitory suburb and the town center are contrasting places.

But within modern cities, the sense of place may decay. There are urban "townscapes" consisting of back lanes, empty lots, railway tracks, and other "spaces between," which lose their saliency as places; they degrade to what Marc Augé, in a famous pun, calls "non-places" (*non-lieux*). When these become large and widespread enough, they drain the city's quality as a place in which other places nest. But human beings need place: to live in, to relate to, to identify with, to feel at home in, and to be able to return to. One of the most important and creative urban projects consists in reclaiming place out of a scatter of non-places, making them again living centers of community life.

This is a facet of the achievement of those who made Market Creek Plaza, which is of great human and also political importance. It is an achievement which has itself something of the nature of an artistic creation, and in turn artistic creations further specify the meaning of a place, they lend this visibility and éclat, and express its relation to those who inhabit it. Moreover, the artistic and cultural expression of communities from many origins helps to integrate multicultural cities.[6]

According to the organizers of Market Creek Plaza, one of the most important lessons to emerge from the project is that helping to build and sustain community engagement and ownership of change requires knowing the questions rather than providing answers. Writing on behalf of JFF and JCNI, president and CEO Jennifer Vanica reflects:

> We abandoned our preconceived notions about
> what people need—and what foundations
> do—and asked people what changes they

---

6 Ashley Graves Lanfer and Madeleine Taylor, *Immigrant Engagement in Public Open Space: Strategies for the New Boston,* last modified December 2010, https://www.barrfoundation.org/blog/immigrant-engagement-in-public -open-space.

For the role of art in creating and empowering public spaces, which also thus become "places," see Christine Bernier and Aube Billard, "Democratic Agendas and the Art World" (presentation to conference on "Democratic Agendas," organized by the Centre for Transcultural Studies together with the Istanbul Policy Center, Istanbul, June 19–20, 2015).

wanted to see and how to go about it . . . We
learned that for community revitalization to be
sustaining, residents must "own their own
change"—the planning, the implementation,
and ultimately the assets. We must work beside
them, encouraging the creativity that results
from their knowledge and love of their own
neighborhoods. This is how a vision is born,
skills are built, and value that benefits them is
created.[7]

The goal in both the Wisconsin and the San Diego
initiatives—intentionally on the part of investors and
facilitators—was to conceive a concrete project (that
was imaginable to residents and, practically speaking,
realizable) as a vehicle for jumpstarting local democracy. Key here is that as a result of broad-based participation in decision-making, there came a fuller recognition among residents and between residents
and outside actors about what residents genuinely
wanted, which led to the development of stronger relationships and alliances. Relationships were mobi-
lized in the context of the projects but survived as
community assets that could be deployed in future

---

7 Robinson et al., *Market Creek Plaza.*

deliberations about local development. Further, more and better information was infused into local discussions, leaving residents with an enhanced capacity for civic engagement and a larger appetite for becoming involved.

The Lawrence CommunityWorks (LCW) network in Lawrence, Massachusetts, is a somewhat different case. Here, a stronger capacity for civic action is being built by linking large numbers of residents in a formally incorporated network. The network is an open environment that allows residents to connect in many ways and for many purposes. The idea is that strong social capital and a web of connections can serve as a platform for developing new leadership, resident engagement, and change in a city.[8]

The impetus for the creation of the network came from LCW, a local Community Development

---

8 Creating networks as platforms for generating multiple, ongoing kinds of social change is gaining currency as a strategy for confronting complex problems that won't yield to a "silver-bullet" solution. See Peter Plastrik, Madeleine Taylor, and John Cleveland, *Connecting to Change the World: Harnessing the Power of Networks for Social Impact* (Washington, DC: Island Press, 2014).

Corporation (CDC) that provides services and resources to mainly low-income residents. Lawrence, a former textile center, is one of the poorest urban centers in the United States. The city lost nearly half its manufacturing jobs in the 1970s and 1980s and a further 20 percent of its employment base in the recession of the early 1990s. Home to increasing numbers of immigrants, Lawrence has a current population of 75,000 and is majority Latinx. LCW's leaders, including a cadre of seasoned organizers and MIT urban planning graduates, recognized that the city's daunting challenges could not be overcome without the involvement of large numbers of residents. Deficits included not only a lack of community assets, such as public infrastructure and effective schools, but also a lack of civic leadership. This was partly because mill owners and other members of the city's former elite did not live in the city itself and left no legacy of civic engagement. LCW leaders concluded that, in order to be successful and sustainable in the long run, transformation in the city would have to start at the base. Then they proposed to do something that is unconventional for a CDC: facilitate a process that would get thousands of residents to talk about and work on local issues, build their leadership skills, and connect locally to change their city.

LCW began by supporting a loose set of affiliations among residents that focused on individual projects, such as building and maintaining a neighborhood playground or taking back abandoned alleyways. This built a track record of success that attracted more residents to community meetings and other organizing efforts. People who were interested in supporting a broader range of projects began to step forward, leading to more comprehensive revitalization efforts in some neighborhoods. At the same time, residents expressed interest in neighborhood programs for youth and financial literacy and English classes, which led to the creation and expansion of LCW services for families. A few years later when staff took stock, they realized that all of this LCW-supported activity was producing direct benefits for residents; it was also producing a lot of connectivity. At this point building a network—connecting people across network clusters, groups, committees, and community institutions—became an intentional part of LCW practice.

"Network building means that development [of the city] is about building a human relationship community infrastructure that can, in turn, produce a bricks-and-mortar infrastructure," said Bill Traynor, LCW's director.[9] Out of the evolving network would come civic leadership and concrete changes in community conditions.

LCW took a deliberate approach to building the network itself. Anyone who lives or works in Lawrence can become a member of the LCW network. And, once in the network, people have many opportunities to become involved. Some activities are principally designed to build social capital, such as residents coming together to share a home-cooked meal. Other activities grow out of organizing efforts, such as "Our Money, Our Future, Our Right to Know," an effort to get more residents involved in discussions about a vision for the community and how local government can best invest its resources to improve the quality of life in Lawrence's neighborhoods. Traynor explains, "What matters is that there are a lot of different doors. Once you get in, you know you are in a network; you can look around and see other things you can participate in, and you can get the culture. People who will come in through one kind of door, wouldn't

---

9 Peter Plastrik and Madeleine Taylor, *Lawrence CommunityWorks: Using the Power of Networks to Restore A City* (Barr Foundation, March 2004), 3.

typically come in through another. This is transformative, the genesis of new orientations and identities upon which future action can be built."[10]

What can this approach produce? Here are some examples:

LCW's "neighbor circles" organizing strategy now involves hundreds of network members as volunteers in neighborhood projects and local community development efforts.

Dozens of residents have been trained as local organizers through the PODER Leadership Institute to become community leaders working to engage other residents in improving the quality of life in their city.

With LCW, residents developed "Our Money, Our Future, Our Right to Know" into "The People's Guide to the Lawrence City Budget," a seventy-two-page bilingual publication that sheds light on the city's three major budgets—operating, capital improvement, and Community Development Block Grants and HOME funds. It explains where the money comes from for each budget, what it funds, who decides how it's spent, and what opportunities there are for residents to get involved.

---

10 Plastrik and Taylor, 5.

Since the creation of the network, LCW has generated over $70 million in new neighborhood investment, including 162 units of affordable housing on fifteen abandoned and vacant parcels, a new community center, three new playgrounds, and a range of family-asset building and youth-development efforts.

LCW has emerged as a major force for equitable development and economic justice in Lawrence, and one of the most dynamic and effective CDCs in Massachusetts. The LCW network already includes thousands of residents who are exploring ways to get involved with one another and with local projects. The LCW network is open and adaptive with activities and a membership that are changing over time. That is one of the advantages of organizing at the base in this way. Rather than focusing on a narrow outcome, the network is generative—it has an enduring capacity to engage and mobilize. Members are deliberate about building, strengthening, and maintaining ties so that they can be activated again and again in different ways depending on the challenge or the opportunity.

The projects discussed in the previous sections were initiated by citizens (often with the support of foun-

dations) rather than by governments. They are examples of self-organizing at the level of local communities. But governments can also initiate consultation
on particular questions with ordinary citizens, not
only on local levels, but also on state or federal levels.
In the last several decades, many democratic innovations have been proposed, in academic discussions as
well as in politics, and many have also been tested in
practice, such as Citizen Councils, Citizens' Assemblies, deliberative polls, or participatory budgeting.
What they have in common is that they are dialogue-
based, participatory modes of consultation that accompany and inform the more traditional processes
of representative democracy.

Before examining specific examples of such projects, we must look briefly at the wider field of democratic participation and policymaking. In many parts
of the Western world, citizens' declining interest in
traditional forms of participation through political
parties and elections is countered by a reassuring increase in the significance of new forms of participation. It is no longer sufficient for people to hand over
control to political decision makers at each election;
they want to join in the conversation and not be
reduced to mere onlookers. For them, it is about
debating alternatives and reclaiming the scope for

political action. More than ever, citizens want to engage in shaping the circumstances of their lives, whether with regard to urban districts, local communities, or regions, or to plans for the public sphere. They are searching for new modes of political participation and demand direct involvement—with increasing success.

Since the 1990s there has been a significant increase in the practice of innovative forms of citizen participation. They have yet to be conclusively defined—in contrast to fully constituted, legally regulated forms of participation such as the consultations that take place in the framework of planning procedures, or the classical mechanisms of direct democracy such as referendums or public petitions conducted at a local authority level.

A considerable number of these new, dialogue-based forms of participation offer proof of this trend—from the Citizens' Assembly in Ireland (for example, on popular aging or climate change) or the one that promoted electoral reform in British Columbia, Canada, through to the consensus conferences convened in Denmark for the purposes of technological assessment, to local initiatives that supported civic engagement in the policymaking of the Keralan government in India. Such processes, which often involve several rounds and depend on the support of facilitators and, potentially, experts (whether academic or otherwise), are geared toward carving out common policy solutions that incorporate a responsible (or "open") attitude toward the future—that is, beyond short-term (election campaign) interests. Citizens are increasingly seizing the opportunity to participate in order to articulate their concerns and influence local, regional, or national policy. Additionally, online tools and technologies have become available over the last decade, allowing larger numbers of citizens to mobilize. Although the "participatory revolution" that began in the 1970s has suffered repeated setbacks, fundamentally it has provided a remedy to the alienation that citizens have expressed with varying degrees of intensity in relation to traditional institutions of democracy in all OECD states.

The spectrum of dialogue-based forms of participation that have been tried to date around the world is large indeed (for a large collection of examples, see participedia.net). Variants range from large-scale town hall meetings with several thousand participants to formations such as citizen councils, planning cells, and consensus conferences with between ten and thirty citizens. Around twenty dialogue-based procedures and methods have now established themselves—complemented by a growing number of online and internet-supported participatory processes. These different forms distinguish themselves from one another according to duration (from a single day to several months) and the number of participants (from ten to several thousand), as well as in the way participating citizens are recruited and selected (self-selection, random, or targeted selection). Some methods (for example, the future workshop) are as a matter of principle open to anyone interested in a particular issue, and participants make a conscious decision to engage in a participatory process. As a result, people with higher levels of formal education and individuals or groups with more leisure time, such as retirees and students, may be disproportionately represented at such workshops. This is also true of those enthusiasts who are sometimes derisively referred to as "the usual suspects" or "professional citizens." While this is not intended as a criticism of particularly active citizens, it is clear that the random recruitment methods used in participatory methods such as wisdom councils or consensus conferences help to ensure that they are not dominated by particular interests. On the other hand, a targeted approach to recruitment (as practiced in mediation) enables organizers to invite particular individuals or representatives of different groups.

The whole spectrum of procedures of consultation might be relevant for a reconstruction of democracy from the bottom up. But again, we want to restrict our discussion here to cases with which we are familiar, and which proved specifically effective in contexts where citizens had to initially define a problem rather than just find a solution to a given problem. The creative potential and focus on the common good that well-executed participation processes can unleash is quite astonishing, and for career politicians who engage with such processes this cooperative approach to policymaking can prove to be an eye-opening experience. Successful citizen participation reveals the various aspects of a problem or conflict, as well as the different principles and values that feed into it, thereby overcoming false consensuses and the depoliticizing narratives of today's party politics. Done properly, citizen participation lends expression to the diversity of opinion and taps into citizens' creativity in developing previously unimagined solutions. This is achieved by allowing people to contrast their views with those of other citizens and to relativize their positions without necessarily abandoning them.

We now look at some interesting experiences.

A project in Bregenz, Austria, offers a good example of dialogue-oriented participation of citizens. Urban-development processes usually unfold within a closely controlled environment and are subject to many and often powerful interests and equally numerous regulatory constraints. In 2009, after several decades of political deadlock, the city council in Bregenz was finally able to put the finishing touches on a master plan to develop a large waterfront area. To ensure that it had the backing of citizens and to provide an avenue for their input in the planning phase, the city council convened a "civic" or "wisdom" council, a model of participatory politics often referred to as the "Voralberg model."[11] It soon became clear that, from the citizens' point of view, the legion of planners commissioned by the city had made a cardinal error. While none of the citizens randomly se-

---

[11] A fuller description of the model can be found in the next section on the civic council convened on refugees.

lected to serve on the council held any relevant professional qualifications, they all recognized that the
project offered a historic opportunity to bridge the
divide between Lake Constance and the city of Bregenz, which were separated by a railway line and a
busy road.

The wisdom council went on to develop a variety
of proposals, including one for a broad pedestrian
overpass serving as a public space ("Spanish Steps"),
which met with the unanimous approval of the city
council. This example demonstrates the capacity of
public participation to harness local knowledge in
the interest of the common good. Rather than serving
as the mouthpiece of a special interest group (wanting
to build shops in this area), the citizens' council ar-
ticulated the thinking of a broad (yet often silent)
and diverse public about the future of their city—this,
in defiance of the ubiquitous trends of gentrification,
degeneration, and social alienation.

Efforts led by nonprofits in the United States are
also creating platforms that engage residents directly
in public policymaking, mainly at a state or local
level. One example is Oregon's Kitchen Table (OKT).
The creation of a group of nonpartisan, nonprofit
community organizations, OKT facilitates in-depth
public deliberations to chart avenues forward on

challenging issues facing the state. OKT links residents to inclusive, fact-based discussions that yield useful recommendations. A recent example is city-wide engagement in setting guidelines for the cleanup of Portland Harbor. Resident values and perspectives that were surfaced and communicated through the process, including the considerations of representatives from multiple racial ethnic groups and refugees, informed state-level environmental priorities and, ultimately, the US Environmental Protection Agency's initial funding allocations for a Portland Harbor Superfund Cleanup. Similar processes have unfolded in locations such as Eau Claire (Wisconsin), Portsmouth (New Hampshire), and Fort Collins (Colorado), signaling a growing demand for the formalization of new approaches to policy formation.

Vivid examples of successful citizen participation at the national level are so-called citizens' assemblies. One of the first took place in British Columbia, Canada, in 2004, when 161 randomly selected citizens were invited to discuss a possible change of the electoral system. The Citizens' Assembly on Electoral Reform was composed of one female and one male member from each of the seventy-nine electoral districts, two representatives of the natives / aboriginals, and one chairman. The selection procedure took into account a representative distribution according to gender, geographical distribution, and age. After the members were determined by a public lottery, the Assembly started in January 2004. The work process had three main phases. In a twelve-week "learning phase," expert lectures and group discussions were held to give members broad access to relevant information. The focus was a critical discussion of existing electoral systems. In a second phase, from May to June, the members held over fifty public lectures on the findings gathered during the first phase. In the third phase, from September to October, members came together again to discuss which electoral system would best be suited for British Columbia in terms of fairness of representation, local representation, and voter choice. In the end, three possible electoral systems emerged, which were balanced against one another in three rounds of elections. After a decision process lasting a year, the Assembly decided on the Single Transferable Vote (STV) system. On December 10, 2004, the final report was presented to the government with a recommendation of changing the electoral system to STV. Although the STV failed in a public referendum the following year because of a missed quorum, it demonstrated how citizen participation can function at larger political scales.

This democratic experiment in Canada became the model for the Irish Citizens' Assembly, which eventually led to a constitutional amendment on the divisive issue of same-sex marriage in 2015. After the economic crisis of 2008, political reforms had become indispensable in Ireland. With the help of the Atlantic Philanthropies Foundation, political scientists David Farrell and Jane Suiter organized a citizens' meeting in June 2011 under the title "We the Citizens." For the first time, one hundred Irish citizens met under the leadership of a professional team of facilitators and discussed questions on reform and tax policy in Ireland. Surprisingly, citizens argued against tax reduction in their final report. Subsequently, the results of the first assembly were passed on to parliamentarians, including the idea of a nationally organized citizens' assembly. The newly elected Fine Gael and Labour Party government agreed to convene a state-initiated citizens' assembly on constitutional reform issues. In July 2012, eight major topics were defined by parliamentary resolution, including climate change and abortion. Tom Arnold, who was chairman of the Irish NGO Concern at the time, became the chairman of the newly established Convention on the Constitution. He was assisted by Art O'Leary, who is currently secretary-general to the Irish President, along with Farrell and Suiter, who provided scientific support for the project. Unlike in the previous assemblies, the government had agreed to appoint thirty-three members of parliament—according to the thirty-three electoral districts—in addition to sixty-six randomly selected citizens (representative in terms of gender, age, and geographic distribution). It was feared that the professionally trained parliamentarians would inappropriately dominate the discussions. In fact, Arnold had to remember time and again that the central criteria for the assemblies' discussion were openness, fairness, and collegiality. "I had to advertise that everyone had the same right to participate," he said (not always successfully, said some citizens).

In April 2013, the Citizens' Assembly decided by secret ballot on extensive proposals for constitutional reforms and the introduction of same-sex marriage. The clear vote of seventy-nine in favor and nineteen against (and one abstention) led Prime Minister Enda Kenny to call for a referendum by the Irish people on same-sex marriage. On May 22, 2015, 62 percent of the Irish people voted for the introduction of same-sex marriage, which required a constitutional amendment. The Irish Citizens' Assembly has shown that even highly controversial issues can be addressed through citizen participation; participants undergo a learning process, and most often change their minds once they have new information or understand other viewpoints. Notwithstanding the skepticism of Irish politics and media, the constructive work of the well-organized and professionally accompanied assemblies managed to prepare political will formation on highly controversial topics at a national level.

Although these examples illustrate the general advance of citizen participation in different places, a broad and systematic institutionalization of citizen participation and the creation of an associated self-evident culture of participation are still missing. There are a few promising initiatives aimed at the gradual institutionalization and development of legal frameworks for citizen participation at a local and regional level. A case in point is the German city of Heidelberg, which has established a municipal coordination office for public participation; this can be regarded as gradual institutionalization of participatory processes at the local level. The range of topics addressed by this office includes urban planning, land use, and climate protection. Its brief and activities are informed by the city's statutory guidelines for public consultation, together with a public list of current planning proposals, which is published online well ahead of the first local council deliberations, thereby enabling citizens to call for greater participation if they feel it is needed. Other regions and many other local authorities are following suit.

Vorarlberg, the westernmost federal state of Austria, incorporated not only direct but also participatory democracy into its constitution in 2013. Vorarlberg then developed a civic council on refugees. In 2015, the State Government of Vorarlberg requested the convention of a civic council by the State Office of Future-Related Issues (Büro für Zukunftsfragen) and a steering committee of actors from civil society, consistent with Vorarlberg's new constitutional framework. The council's task was to reflect upon the asylum and refugee policies in the Vorarlberg region and to discuss questions connected to the sudden rise in refugee numbers (in May 2015, numbers of asylum applications had increased by 250 percent compared to May 2014): How should the region react locally to the global developments that had led to the increased number of asylum applications? What could be done to facilitate the reception of refugees in the region? How could the actions of different actors (refugees, citizens, media, government, and other institutions) be coordinated in response to the new challenges?[12]

To ensure the inclusion of different opinions and lifestyles, the twenty-three members were convened by lot. As a result, the council was diverse in a number of respects: age (eighteen to seventy-five years), gender (twelve male, eleven female), and hometown. In addition, to specifically anchor the perspective of refugees and asylum seekers in the process, it was guaranteed that at least 20 percent of the members of the civic council had to have either a background as a refugee or a family background of migration.

As a first step, the civic council worked out a joint statement in a closed session over two days. Deliberations were structured by four facilitators familiar with the method of Dynamic Facilitation to ensure a constructive, creative collaboration among the participants. Most notably, the joint statement offered a detailed reflection of the general conditions for successful coexistence; it stressed the importance of opportunities for contact between the local population and refugees and that the independence of refugees

---

12 The full civic council report, including quotes from participants, can be found at https://dk-media.s3.amazonaws.com/AA/AL/diapraxis /downloads/297775/Doku_BR_Asyl1-Engl-EndVers.pdf; a shorter process description can be found at https://participedia.net/case/5383.

needed to be strengthened by facilitating entry to the labor market. In addition, it elaborated practical steps required to realize those conditions, such as the recognition of the asylum seekers' education and training or the identification of easily accessible, suitable jobs in the region.

When asked about their experience during this first stage of the council, participants reported that they had together felt that "everyone can make a difference, can do something" and "this concerns us all!" They also felt that the setup of the workshop had encouraged them to focus on practical solutions instead of fears and misgivings and that it had made them more open to new information, which, in turn, had helped them to unlearn old prejudices. Finally, the members who did not have a personal history of migration reported that the discussion had made them more curious and more concerned about the fate of refugees and migrants and that, as a result, they also cared more about them now. Thus, even at this initial stage of the process, within the limited time frame of two days, the civic council provided an occasion for the development of our four building blocks of deliberative communities outlined in Chapter 1: the construction of a collective sense of agency on the community level, inclusive solidarities and trust, collective creativity, and the alignment of goals and knowledge.

To diffuse the results and the experiences of the civic council more widely in the regional community, the first step of the process was supplemented by further steps. A couple of days after the initial round of the civic council, the steering committee set up two "civic cafés," public fora at which the joint statement of the civic council was presented, explained, and discussed. These public meetings not only helped gain wide acceptance for the proposals of the joint statement, but also contributed to the sense of collective agency and responsibility that had been fostered in the civic council within the local community. Participants expressed this sense by claiming, for example, "it's all about attitude and the willingness to help, of finding a way to deal with the development that reduces fear."

As a third stage in the process, a responder team met in July to review the results of the preceding stages and to develop solutions on the institutional level. The responder team consisted of representatives of institutions responsible for handling the refugee and asylum issues on the administrative level, as well as a group of people who had been involved either in setting up the civic council process (representatives of the State Office of Future-Related Issues, members of the steering committee) or had taken part in the civic council itself (one of the members and one of the facilitators). The tasks of the responder team were twofold: First, they tried to coordinate the activities and responsibilities of the institutions to handle the asylum and refugee issues more effectively and in line with the recommendations of the civic council. Second, they responded to the call for the facilitation of volunteering opportunities on the level of the local community. This third stage of the process was crucial to transfer the ideas of the civic council to concrete policies and actions.

Notably, the "Vorarlberg model" not only includes a constitutional framework for civic councils, but also takes account of the fact that civic consultation needs to be carefully designed with regard to both the internal structure of deliberations (as by the use of methods of facilitation or by designing a process with various stages) and the connection to political and administrative bodies.

Even though these attempts to institutionalize and consolidate citizen participation within a broader framework are promising, the potential of participatory democracy is in general still limited by an established logic, pertaining to both thought and action, that accompanies representative politics. From the side of politicians and civil servants, the main obstacle we still encounter is the absence of openness to and readiness for change, scarcity of resources (both money and personnel), anxiety, and resistance, as well as a lack of knowledge about participatory processes. But one thing is certain: the desire for participation and the readiness of citizens for political engagement is there and will not dwindle in the foreseeable future. Politicians and civil servants must grasp that they can channel this engagement into constructive outcomes oriented toward the general good—and thus strengthen their own legitimacy as representatives—or it will express itself increasingly in unrest, protest, and political stalemate.

Citizen participation will not only help to revitalize our democracies. It might also enhance the problem-solving capacities of representative democracies with regard to problems like transformations toward sustainability. Such transformations need dialogue-based processes that are not only about the weighing up of specific properties and benefits (for example wind versus solar power) but making fundamental decisions as to the general direction of development of a whole society. They touch upon issues concerning quality of life, dominant life-styles and their alternatives, place-making concepts, and so on. Contrary to impressions, or to how things may seem to the politicians, administrators, and business people who initiate energy transformations (or transformations toward a more sustainable future), this is a project of concern not only to engineers and experts; it entails substantial social and political mobilization and is therefore "everybody's project." Citizens should, for example, be enabled to collaborate effectively with regard to the application of the strategy for phasing out coal in a local community or region. A much more comprehensive discussion of our economic model might be required as well, especially regarding its dependency on its concept of gainful employment and such a high volume of resources. One might, for example, discuss a social and ecological economic policy as an alternative to a Keynesian policy geared toward growth, as well as the need to reduce consumption. Such questions cannot, of course, be couched in highly abstract terms; they have to be weighed up with references to concrete examples of specific local and regional projects.

It is not so much technological innovations that need discussing but the future of society at large; that is, not simply how a given urban population can drastically reduce carbon emissions during the course of the next couple of decades, but rather the kind of lives people wish to lead ten or thirty years hence, and the overall direction in which they would like to develop. There must therefore be a sufficient level of citizen participation that makes perspectives on the mid- to long-term future the center of attention, and that leads to their expression in a fitting discursive form, such that this discourse is picked up by legislative and executive bodies. In short, a discourse that ensures such perspectives form a basis for decision making.

To this end, Claus Leggewie and Patrizia Nanz have proposed a "future council," a permanent body that is tasked with identifying important future-oriented questions and potential solutions.[13] These councils consist of fifteen to fifty randomly selected persons, providing a representative sample of the local population, in particular with respect to its generational mix. The council should convene regularly,

13 Patrizia Nanz and Claus Leggewie, *No Representation Without Consultation: A Citizen's Guide to Participatory Democracy* (Toronto: Between the Lines, 2019).

and its members should receive a modest allowance to cover expenses during their two-year term of office. A team of administrative assistants with experience in facilitation should support the operation and management of the council.

The creation of a network of future councils spanning the various levels of the political landscape—from the municipal to the regional, country, and European level—could contribute to efforts to address challenges posed by the interaction of local and higher-level entities (multilevel governance challenges) and global problems that can only be addressed at the local level. To put a new spin on a commonplace of US politics (and the "glocalization" of our world in a nutshell), all politics is local and has global effects.

The proposed future councils would provide an ongoing means to address long-term challenges and projects (that is, those with planning horizons at least ten years distant) that are likely to affect future generations (including today's under-twenties)—even if possible conflicts of interest are not yet manifest. This focus has the potential to counterbalance the "presentism" that is characteristic of contemporary politics, in which actors always have their eyes on the next election, the last poll, or a looming quarterly review.

There is no shortage of topics that could be addressed. These include the transformation of a coal region or the transformation of business and society through the adoption of digital information and communication technologies, which will have far-reaching consequences for employment, privacy, and politics (and for diverse forms of public participation).

Future councils must be designed with a view to maintaining group cohesion, preventing the emergence of cliques, facilitating effective and fair communication, and promoting creative group processes. To achieve this, future councils should comprise no more than fifteen to twenty participants at the local level, and up to fifty participants at the state and federal levels. In order to properly reflect the population's heterogeneous composition, the council members should be chosen through a process of qualified random selection. Ensuring the fair and equal representation of all age groups and balance of gender should be a primary concern. It is equally important that future councils bring together citizens with different educational backgrounds and that migrants are also adequately represented.

An administrative team and facilitators should provide a supportive framework, safeguarding the quality of communications and enabling citizens to largely organize their work processes independently. The implementation of mandatory feedback mechanisms linking local councils, state legislatures, and the federal parliament with future councils will be crucial to the success of this model of public participation. These mechanisms must provide transparency as to whether and how issues raised by future councils are addressed. The adoption of these mechanisms would impose a duty on decision-making bodies to justify their actions (or lack thereof) to future councils, municipalities, and entire regions, and not only in the present moment, but in the months and years following. This duty must be included in the relevant rules of procedure in order to encourage future councils, the public, and political leaders to engage in meaningful dialogue on equal terms. The obligation placed on future councils to report on their activities at regular intervals is paralleled by the requirement that the executive and legislative branches consider and respond within a reasonable period. In case the findings and recommendations of a future council have a significant impact on the political process, the electorate could be asked to voice its opinion in a referendum.

In referring to the consultative (the network of future councils and temporary forms of citizen participation around specific planning processes or decisions) as the fourth power, we strive not to erode the democratic separation of powers or indeed representative democracy itself—whether by technocratic or revolutionary means—but to support both through the wisdom of the many at the base in a contemporary and decentralized form. The consultative can, to a certain extent, compensate for the shortcomings of previous democratic bodies. By providing a forum for the articulation of value conflicts, for example, future councils can offset the growing depoliticization of party politics and prevent well-organized stakeholders from dominating decision-making around key issues affecting our future—the growing power exercised by private investors in the urban-development process springs to mind here (together with the cronyism and corruption for which the industry is known).

In addition, future councils can relieve pressure on overstretched political actors by sharing responsibility for long-term or high-risk decisions and bringing to bear both the diversity of their representatives and their constructive wisdom in the process. By facilitating cooperation among citizens, politicians, experts, and government agencies, future councils can significantly expand the scope for political action and strengthen representative democracy as a whole—but only if established political institutions are willing to grant citizens a meaningful role in addressing future challenges, engage in genuine dialogue, and guarantee to provide clear feedback in response to the public's input.[14]

Before closing this discussion of successful projects of citizen participation, we should envision how the expansion of participation might improve the fate of a community like the one in the Lusatia (Lausitz) region in the former East Germany, where there has been large-scale coal extraction for a long time. At the national level, namely between the ministries, there is an emerging consensus that, especially in East German states, an energy transition is needed, for obvious reasons in view of the present critical condition of the planet. However, in the Lusatia region

---

14 Notably, there is an intersection with the Wisconsin case, as Incourage and other local stakeholders seek to engage state-level officials in the further elaboration and financing of the Tribune project. Though not a future council process, this is evidence of the convergence of ground-up community deliberations and public sector decision making.

itself the relative consensus on a phaseout of coal is contested.

The situation here is analogous to that of Appalachia in the United States. The region will have to adjust to the loss of a significant share of its local economic activities. For workers and individuals in local communities, there are questions of identity linked to their existing professional lives as well as the social and family networks that depend economically on mining. Previous coal transitions in many parts of the world have focused on technical rather than on social or political aspects of structural change, managing the consequences of coal closure rather than proactively addressing the uncertainty of the people and empowering them to develop a coherent vision and alternative strategy for their region.

In Germany, the federal government and the Länder (the states) recently came up with a sizeable fund for the Lausitz. The draft for a new federal law (August 2019) budgets for around seventeen billion euros in subsidies for infrastructure and economic development in the region until 2038.[15] The prime

---

15 Bundesministeriums für Wirtschaft und Energie, *Entwurf eines Strukturstärkungsgesetzes Kohleregionen,* August 2019, https://www.bmwi.de /Redaktion/DE/Downloads/E/entwurf-eines-strukturstaerkungsgesetzes -kohleregionen.pdf?__blob=publicationFile&v=10.

ministers of Saxony and Brandenburg have issued a list with seventy projects—a quick railway to Berlin, an initiative fostering tourism in the Lausitz, and the establishment of new research institutes in the region, for example—vaguely assuming that these projects will regenerate the region economically, but without knowing if these projects are truly in the long-term collective interest of the population. On closer look, there are conflicting perspectives of the matter at stake. Is it about jobs, the development of innovative business locations, or regional identity? Or even national identity? For the regional transformation to succeed, it cannot be just about receiving money; it must also involve regional actors and the people interested in being an active part of the regional transformation. To this end, we need well-organized and genuine citizen participation. So, in spite of the many conflicts, the main questions are as follows: How can local communities be encouraged to take their fate in hand? And what should collaboration involving regional actors in the definition of the policy problems and the formulation of future avenues look like? However, citizen participation must be connected to political institutions and become a kind of operating system for a new political architecture of regional transformations. It would

appear that the situation calls out for the kind of coherent project that we described earlier in this chapter
in our discussion of SWC. But as yet none seems to
be on the horizon.

Many people today live in a state of self-imposed iso-
lation, turning their backs on politics or forming new
identity- and interest-based communities. The consultative approach proposed here would create a
sphere of institutionalized participation to ensure
that citizens' fundamental beliefs, and where they
come into conflict, are acknowledged and harnessed
for the public good. This sphere must be about how we
shape our common future and is no place for vague
promises. The legislative and executive branches
of democratic government must be required to state
whether and to what effect the results of participatory consultation will be taken into account in the
political process. This does not imply that the consultative process ought to be given the same weight
as the decision-making power of the elected representatives. Our point of reference here is Hannah Arendt's concept of the political sphere, invoked above,
which underscores the importance of common action

in public space in contrast to the actions of politicians or the social system of government or administration. Arendt's theory emphasizes the political rationality that is manifest in communicative experiences of common deliberation that transcend everyday human relations. This dimension of the ideal and continuously unfolding political life is a reminder that it is our role as citizens to create this shared space for democratic self-determination.

The institutionalization of citizen participation, such as of future councils, is an important step toward the establishment of a participatory democracy. This would give momentum to a broad process of social learning and mark a shift in the normative framework of collective action with the capacity to transform the political system. It will not be enough to merely add a thin facade of participation to a largely depoliticized democratic system. Rather, what is needed is a change in the very modus of democratic politics.

CHAPTER 3

Contributing to Democratic Renewal

IT MIGHT HELP to draw together the threads that have been running through this description of rather diverse projects on several continents. Two basic goals animate all of these initiatives, however different they are in architecture and mode of operation: (1) to define new and potentially fruitful policies or programs to meet important needs of citizens, and (2) to create commitment, cohesion, or solidarity around these policies. Despite different approaches to achieving these objectives, all of the projects share these goals.

The projects of self-organization at the base that we discussed Chapter 2 advance these aims together, whereas some of the modes of consultation we looked at are more effective in defining new solutions than in mobilizing support for them. Then again, the latter projects ensure a more representative sample of the population than volunteer recruitment, which tends to initially attract traditional elites. In any case, well-crafted solutions to recalcitrant problems will draw support. (See the case of Bregenz in Chapter 2, and the way in which consultation can morph into active participation in decision-making, as in the case of Vorarlberg.)

Together, these two aims serve the crucial goal we outlined in Chapter 1: reconnecting citizens with their needs and aspirations to our representative institutions, or in other words, enlarging the realm of the political in Hannah Arendt's sense. We believe that without this and other kinds of expansion, our representative democracies are at grave risk.

Different as the projects are, we must also note certain common conditions. They usually require two kinds of input from outside, either from governments or from nonprofits and foundations. The first input is the initiative to get the project going: for instance, a government that sets up a future council and oversees the selection of its members, or a foundation, like Incourage in Wisconsin or the Jacobs Center for Neighborhood Innovation in San Diego. This often requires considerable funding, on a scale that the community itself is unable or (at the beginning) unwilling to contribute. This funding must be forth-coming over a considerable period of time.

The second input is expertise of various kinds: scientific knowledge, understanding of the economic context, awareness of the pitfalls of this kind of organization, and so on. But—as we have stressed throughout—such expertise cannot be delivered from on high and from the stance of "we know and you're ignorant," especially in the current climate of suspicion and hostility toward elites. Failure to take this factor into account can undermine the entire project and condemn it to failure. This second input can only be mediated by skilled facilitators who understand this suspicion of elites and can win the confidence of the people and communities who are seeking an effective voice. Their role is crucial to reconstructing democracy from the ground up.

We now return briefly to our background concern for the critical condition of contemporary democracies, which we expressed at the outset. How can strengthening democracy at the base, in its various forms, contribute to reviving democracy at the level of the whole polity? How can it contribute to both the feeling and the reality of citizen efficacy? How can it help overcome or bypass the failings of our representative systems?

To answer these questions, we have to look at what has been happening in these systems in recent decades. In theory, citizens can have influence by voting for a party that promises to enact the voters' wishes. By joining a party and working within it to determine its program, a citizen can ensure that the party is proposing favorable goals. Arguably, this idealization of the political process was never fully realized, but in Western democracies we were certainly closer to it fifty years ago than we are today. Since then, numerous political issues have become increasingly complex and often intractable; we need mention only the most dramatic global developments, like climate change and mass intercontinental migrations, but many other issues arise from automation, mass communications, social media, greater diversity, and the like. Meanwhile, multiple political parties have been established in many countries, largely in response to these new issues; green parties are a good example. These new options have often contributed to the decline of traditional parties.

These two changes make it difficult for citizens to find a party that promises to realize their favored goals across a range of issues, and even if such a party exists, it will need to work alongside others to pass the required legislation. These two developments have contributed to the opacity and seeming inaccessibility of representative democracies that have undermined the sense of citizen efficacy, but the reverse is also the case: citizen participation in the party system has fallen off dramatically in many cases, contributing to the weakness of parties and their failure to reflect citizens' opinions and aspirations. This cyclical causality, a downward spiral of the party system, becomes a problem for representative government itself.

How to respond to this? How to recover confidence in representative democracy? We must look to other developments in our democracies, and in particular to citizens' movements, which can agitate, lead campaigns, and organize demonstrations, often on a mass scale, to demand certain measures from governments. Examples from recent years include the various Occupy movements, the *Indignados* movement in Spain, and the recent mobilizations of school students to demand changes in gun legislation in the United States.

These movements are powerful, but they often fail to bring about the changes that they aim for because of a lack of coordination with the representative system, political parties, legislators, and governments. This lack is motivated by a disdain on the part of the demonstrators for politicians, whom they view as motivated by base interest, which is answered by an equal and opposite patronizing attitude on the part of politicians for naïve and starry-eyed youngsters.

The result is that the worthy goals of movements like Occupy—striving to put curbs on the power of banks to throw the whole economy into a tailspin, as in 2008—are frustrated, to everyone's great disadvantage. Both parties and movements have to coordinate their action, or both risk being powerless to influence the course of events. In effect, what earlier parties often managed to achieve through their abundant membership and their links with trade unions and cooperatives, channeling mass sentiment into legislative proposals, now has to be recreated by forging alliances between parties and movements. This synergy, essential to achieving meaningful change, can no longer be assured by the very structure of institutions, as with the social-democratic parties of yore, but needs to be created afresh in each new predicament by concerted action.

But what does this have to do with the modes of democracy at the base that we have been discussing? It should be obvious that the collaboration of such local initiatives with broader movements for change could make an important difference to the success of the latter. Their clarity on what they need can both strengthen the larger movements for change and render their goals more defined and better informed. They can recruit participants and give them additional grounds and arguments for their demands. In this they can and should work alongside organizations engaged in advocacy, bringing expertise to support certain reforms.

Imagine the synergy created if these three kinds of action—parties, social movements, and highly informed and solidly committed local community and advocacy organizations—were brought into alignment. Let's look again at one of the cases with which this book started: the situation of certain rust belt regions, where earlier forms of employment have dried up and people feel bitter and neglected. This powerful negative emotion has helped fuel the campaigns of Donald Trump in the United States and Marine Le Pen in France, for instance. But what would have happened if these regions had already been through the kind of search for alternative economic vocations that we described, if a consensus had been formed around the best direction to go, if therefore the emptiness of the promises of these demagogues to restore a past greatness had been shown up? It is not too great a stretch to imagine the mobilization of a greater movement around this consensus program on the part of all those who are horrified by the xenophobic, divisive campaigns of these highly destructive figures.

In effect, we have here the sketch of a democratic counterblow against the current drift to stagnation and xenophobic exclusion, which reciprocally strengthen each other. This is the kind of synergy we need to create. Democracy at the base is one of its crucial components.[1]

---

1 James and Deborah Fallows's informative and interesting book, *Our Towns,* documents the rich fund of ideas and entrepreneurial initiatives that exist in a number of local communities in the United States. They regret the fact that these are not complemented by supportive action from the federal government. We very much agree that some synergy between the two is essential to the rebuilding of American democracy. James Fallows and Deborah Fallows, *Our Towns: A 100,000-Mile Journey into the Heart of America* (New York: Pantheon Books, 2018).

Coda

IN THIS BOOK, we deal with the immediate situation of crisis in which our contemporary democracies find themselves, but if we look further into the future, it is likely that organized local communities will have to play an increasingly significant role. Though we cannot be sure, it is possible that globalization and robotization will bring about a further shrinkage of well-paying jobs in the advanced economies of the West. At present, the standard way to ensure full employment in these economies is through continued production growth. The more people lose their jobs in declining industries, the more we have to generate new jobs on the same scale.

This is the case not only because our contemporary societies generally lack imagination, but also because our concept of the useful, contributing citizen is dominated by the producer-for-the-market—the worker or entrepreneur who can produce something consumers are willing to buy. It's possible to imagine societies in the developed world receiving immense revenues from abroad for exports generated by largely automated industries; their surplus could then provide a guaranteed annual income for their population, even for those who won't or can't find jobs. By itself, this solution would be unviable, because it would not offer a role that confers a sense of dignity or worth on masses of unemployed recipients of such an income. As it turns out, this shrinking of traditional jobs will take place at the same time as the need for essential human services grows: as our population ages and people retire earlier; as the educational requirements of ordinary jobs become higher; and as the proportion of school children needing special attention increases (based on current trends).

We need a cultural shift in which new forms of occupation that benefit others, but don't involve continued quantitative growth in production or in nonrenewable energy, can become meaningful for large numbers of people. At the same time, essential human services will need more participants. It is obvious that this latter development could be one of our answers to the new need created by the shrinking of regular jobs that used to confer the status of breadwinner.

The new era will require more workers in essential human services, but there will also be opportunities for providing forms of continuing education, training, or development in the arts or in new services. The trainees could earn an income from their skills, but with continuing education, and the arts, the point would mainly be enabling people to live more creative lives, even if that by itself does not generate an income.

We are looking at a need for a great transfer of collective wealth from the production of saleable goods and services to this range of human services. This runs against many of the assumptions of our neoliberal societies, which are always desperately trying to keep collective service costs low and taxes light in order to encourage growth and thus jobs in the private sector. Aside from this radical shift in budgetary priorities, the sharp boundary between paid work and volunteer work may be breached. In many modern societies, important roles in health care and education institutions are now filled by volunteers: for example, supervising children on trips out of school, or helping accompany older people in institutions. These must be filled by volunteers because the official institutions operate on stretched budgets and can't afford to fill these functions with salaried employees.

We imagine a new kind of society beyond breakneck growth, which could soften the dichotomy between salaried employees and volunteers and encourage larger numbers of people through incentives to take part in the kinds of activities now carried out by volunteers. They would basically be volunteers, but some of their expenses might be paid. For instance, imagine a society with some modest guaranteed income; this probably would be inadequate for many people, so they might seek part-time work. But in this imagined world, they might earn a supplement by taking up one of the volunteer functions in a hospital, school, old-age home, or community garden. They would be "incentivized volunteers."

It is clear that such a scheme would have to be handled on the local level, in light of available budgets, and taking into account the gamut of needs in the local health care and education services. Once more, we would need these organized-and-mobilized communities to take their fate in their own hands in order to best serve the needs of their inhabitants, both those using the health care or education services, and those who find a meaningful sense of their lives by contributing to the common good through volunteering.

We can hope that there would no longer be the dichotomous consciousness we now have between those with regular full-time jobs and those who receive social assistance, supported by the taxes levied on job-holders. We would have legitimized other ways of contributing to the common good that blurred this sharp boundary. We might have people who, thanks to their extra formation in some academic subject or art, might get satisfaction from giving free lectures or lessons to the public. There would be a host of in-centivized volunteers along with those who volunteer without needing any subsidy, and then there would be people in part-time and full-time employment. The sense of a sharp boundary would be eroded. Of course, this could not replace the necessary large-scale shift in budgetary priorities, but it could supplement it by ensuring that human needs are fully met.

This all means that we must devise new ways of en-couraging and inciting local communities to take their fate in hand. Building democracy at the base has an essential role in resolving our present crisis, but it will also be an essential part of the more hu-mane, less growth-obsessed society we want to build in the future.

ACKNOWLEDGMENTS

We are very grateful to André Lima for indispensable work in preparing and editing the manuscript, to Simon Meisch for his very valuable comments, and, in particular, to Lukas Kübler for an excellent reorganization of the text. We would also like to thank Aube Billard for accompanying our writing process with flashes of insight and great cheerfulness.

INDEX